Coo Coo For CocoNUTS!

50 Delicious Coconut Recipes!

Samantha Sterling

Recipe Junkies

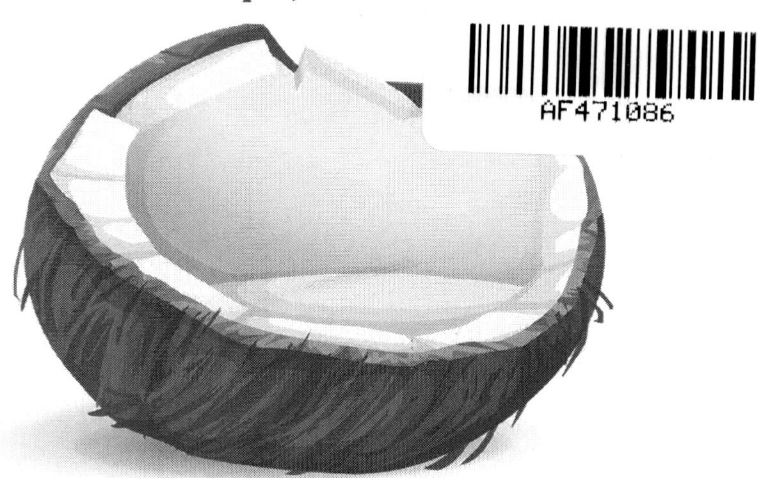

Coconut Oil Buns for Sandwiches

Spaghetti Bolognese Sauce

Black Bean and Quinoa Salad with Cucumber

Sea Bass with Spiraled Courgette and Carrots

Asparagus with New Potato Salad

Butternut Squash with Beetroot Soup and Ginger

Squid with Brown Rice Pasta and Chili Flakes

Cauliflower and Broccoli Cheese Muffins

Thai Red Curry Chicken

Crockpot Red Lentil Curry

Coconut Shrimp and Spicy Peach Dip

Coconut Curry Crispy Fried Chicken

Teriyaki Coconut Chicken

Spaghetti Squash and Shrimp Pesto

Coconut Chicken and Spinach

Peanut and Coconut Chili Chicken

Slow Cooked Peanut Butter Chicken with Ramen Noodles

Paleo Basil with Avocado Zucchini Pasta

Ginataang Langka and Pork

Easy Balsamic Salmon

Crusted Tilapia and Coconut Almonds

Paleo Shepherds Pie

Spinach Coconut Curry

Pina Colada Pork Chops

Chicken Verde Enchiladas

Tomato Basil Coconut Chicken

Teriyaki Salmon

Coconut Curried Rice

Saucy Coconut Green Beans and Chicken

Asian Paleo Chicken Meatballs and Teriyaki Glaze

Ribs in the Slow Cooker

Coconut Sloppy Joe

Coconut Thai Rice

Curry Soup with Coconut, Lime, and Chicken

Lime Coconut Shrimp

Ginger and Coconut rice

Coconut Thai Red Curry

Curried Coconut Chicken

Coconut Shrimp with Sweet and Sour Sauce

Coconut Sweet Potato Coconut Casserole

Coconut Catfish Soup

Coconut Cheese Log

Sticky Coconut Rice

Breaded Coconut Fish

Sour Cream Coconut Cake

Coconut 5-Minute Pie

Coconut Almond Coconut Cookies

Coconut Cream Pie

Chocolate Coconut Pie

Pina Colada (Can be made with no alcohol.)

Thank You!

Coconut Oil Buns for Sandwiches

Ingredients:

- 1 ¼ Cup of Milk – Warmed
- 1 Egg – Beaten
- 2 Tbsp. of Coconut Oil – Soft
- ¼ Cup of Whole Sugar
- ¾ tsp. of Salt
- 2 ¾ Cup of Flour
- 1 Cup of Wheat Flour
- 1 ¼ tsp. of Active Dry Yeast – Not Quick Rising
- 1 Tbsp. of Coconut Oil – Melted

Directions:

1. If you are using a bread machine, put the ingredients (except for 1 Tbsp. of coconut oil)

into your machine in the order that it is listed. Select the Dough setting.

2. When it is finished, turn it out onto a floured board and then roll it out to ½ inch – ¾ inch thickness.

3. Cut it into 3-inch circles.

4. Put them on a lightly greased baking sheet (use coconut oil). Brush the tops with the rest of the coconut oil.

5. Cover it and allow it to rise for about an hour in a warm and draft free area.

6. Bake it at 350 degrees Fahrenheit for 10-15 minutes until they are golden brown.

Nutritional Information:

- Calories: 247
- Total Fat: 12g
- Saturated Fat: 7g
- Carbohydrates: 25g
- Protein: 9g

Spaghetti Bolognese Sauce

Ingredients:

- 14 Ounces of Aberdeen Angus Beef
- 3 Tbsp. of Coconut Oil
- 2 Cloves of Garlic – Crushed
- 2 Onions – Chopped
- ½ Cup of Carrots – Sliced
- ¼ Cup of Celery – Chopped Fine
- 3 Large Tomatoes – Chopped Small
- 1 Tbsp. of Tomato Puree
- Dash of Thyme – Dried
- Dash of Salt
- Dash of Pepper

Directions:

1. Preheat your oven to 300 degrees Fahrenheit.

2. In a large saucepan, add in the coconut oil and heat it up.

3. Add in the onions, celery, carrots, and the garlic. Saute it for 8-10 minutes until they are soft.

4. Increase the heat slightly, add in the mince and stir it until the meat is completely browned.

5. Stir in the tomatoes, tomato puree, thyme, pepper, and salt.

6. Stir everything very well and bring it to a simmer.

Nutritional Information:

- Calories: 224
- Total Fat: 7g
- Saturated Fat: 2g
- Carbohydrates: 35g
- Protein: 5g

Black Bean and Quinoa Salad with Cucumber

Ingredients:

- 1 ½ Cups of Quinoa
- 4 ½ Cups of Water
- 1 tsp. of Coconut Oil
- 1 Red Bell Pepper
- ¼ Cucumber
- 13 Ounces of Black Beans – Drained
- ¼ Cup of Extra Virgin Olive Oil
- 1 tsp. of Ground Cumin
- 1 Clove of Garlic – Crushed
- Juice from ½ Lemon
- Cherry Tomatoes – Quartered
- 1 Handful of Coriander – Chopped

Directions:

1. Add in the quinoa, coconut oil, and the water to a saucepan and then cook it for 15 minutes until all the water is absorbed.

2. Drain the beans and then chop up your pepper and your cucumber into small bits.

3. In a separate mixing bowl, add in the olive oil, garlic, cumin, and the lemon to make the dressing.

4. Once your quinoa is done, mix it in a large mixing bowl with the pepper, beans, and cucumber.

5. Top it with the cherry tomatoes.

6. Drizzle the dressing on the top and garnish it with the coriander.

Nutritional Information:

- Calories: 220
- Total Fat: 2g
- Saturated Fat: 1g
- Carbohydrates: 25g
- Protein: 3g

Sea Bass with Spiraled Courgette and Carrots

Ingredients:

- 1 Large Courgette
- 1 Large Carrot – Peeled
- 1 tsp. of Coconut Oil
- Dash of Chili Flakes
- 2-4 Sea Bass Fillets
- Coriander – Chopped, Garnish

Directions:

1. Spiral your courgette and the carrot.
2. In a heavy pan, heat the coconut oil until it is hot.
3. Add in the chili flakes and the sea bass. Put it in skin side down.
4. After 3 minutes, turn the fillets over and cook it for another 3 minutes. Remove it and put it on a plate.
5. Add in the courgette and the carrots. Stir-fry it for 2 minutes.

6. Remove it from the heat and put it on the plates with the fish on top.

7. Sprinkle the coriander on the top before you serve it.

Nutritional Information:

- Calories: 175
- Total Fat: 4g
- Saturated Fat: 2g
- Carbohydrates: 3g
- Protein: 24g

Asparagus with New Potato Salad

Ingredients:

- 10 Asparagus Stalks
- 8 Baby Potatoes
- 2 Eggs – Hard Boiled
- 10 Cherry Tomatoes
- Handful of Baby Spinach
- 1 Tbsp. of Coconut Oil
- Dash of Salt
- Dash of Pepper

Directions:

1. Preheat your oven to 350 degrees Fahrenheit.
2. Add in half of the coconut oil in a roasting dish and warm it in your oven.

3. Wash your potatoes and then halve them. Toss the coconut oil, seasonings, and the potatoes. Bake them for 30-35 minutes.

4. Add in the rest of the coconut oil to the baking tray. Allow it to melt then toss in the asparagus. Roast it for 10 minutes.

5. Crumble the eggs on a bed of spinach on the plates.

6. Add the tomatoes (halved) on top.

7. Add the asparagus and the potatoes on the plate and serve it.

Nutritional Information:

- Calories: 150
- Total Fat: 7g
- Saturated Fat: 2g
- Carbohydrates: 9g
- Protein: 2g

Butternut Squash with Beetroot Soup and Ginger

Ingredients:

- 1 Ounce of Coconut Oil
- 2 Onions – Chopped
- 1 Squash
- 28 Ounces of Beetroot – Peeled, Chopped. Cooked
- 15 Ounces of Sweet Potato – Peeled, Chopped
- 10 Ounces of Leeks – Chopped
- 2 Cloves of Garlic – Minced
- 1 tsp. of Cinnamon
- 33 Ounces of Stock (Chicken or Vegetable)
- 1 tsp. of Nutmeg
- 1 inch Piece of Ginger – Peeled, Chopped
- Dash of Salt
- Dash of Pepper
- Coriander – Chopped

Directions:

1. Sauté the onions, ginger, and the garlic for 3 minutes on medium heat.
2. Add in the leeks and stir it well for another 5 minutes.
3. Add in the squash, beetroot, and the sweet potatoes. Cover it with the stock.
4. Add in the cinnamon, salt, pepper, and the nutmeg. Stir it.
5. Bring it to a boil, cover it and allow it to simmer for 30-40 minutes until the vegetables are soft.
6. Stir in the chopped coriander and the chili flakes.

Nutritional Information:

- Calories: 120
- Total Fat: 2g
- Saturated Fat: 1g
- Carbohydrates: 18g
- Protein: 3g

Squid with Brown Rice Pasta and Chili Flakes

Ingredients:

- 17 Ounces of Brown Rice Pasta
- 2 Ounces of Coconut Oil
- 17 Ounces of Squid – Rings
- 5 Ounces of Red Onion – Sliced Thin
- ½ tsp. of Crushed Chilies
- 2 Cloves of Garlic – Chopped Fine
- 1 Tbsp. of Sherry Vinegar
- Parsley – Chopped

Directions:

1. Cook the pasta using the instructions on the package.
2. Melt the coconut oil in a large pan.
3. Sauté the onions and then add in the garlic. Cook it for 2-3 minutes. Stir it so that the onions and the garlic are completely mixed together.
4. Add in the squid and the chilies. Cook it for 3-5 minutes. Make sure not to over cook it.

5. Add in the sherry vinegar and the parsley. Stir it well.

Nutritional Information:

- Calories: 246
- Total Fat: 2g
- Saturated Fat: 0g
- Carbohydrates: 45g
- Protein: 9g

Cauliflower and Broccoli Cheese Muffins

Ingredients:

- 2 ½ Ounces of Cauliflower
- 2 ½ Ounces of Broccoli
- 1 ½ Ounces of Cheese – Grated or Shredded
- 1 tsp. of Dijon Mustard
- 5 Eggs
- 1 tsp. of Coconut Oil – Melted
- Dash of Salt
- Dash of Pepper

Directions:

1. Preheat your oven to 350 degree Fahrenheit.
2. Grease the muffin tray with the coconut oil.
3. Put the cooked cauliflower and the broccoli into a muffin case.
4. Whisk the eggs, Dijon mustard, cheese, coconut oil, salt, and the pepper.
5. Pour in equal amounts into the case.
6. Put them in the oven and bake it for 25 minutes.

7. Allow it to cool for 5 minutes.

Nutritional Information:

- Calories: 370
- Total Fat: 14g
- Saturated Fat: 2g
- Carbohydrates: 61g
- Protein: 6g

Thai Red Curry Chicken

Ingredients:

- 1 Tbsp. of Coconut Oil
- ¼ Yellow Onion – Sliced Thin
- ½ Red Pepper – Cut to Matchstick Strips
- ½ Yellow Peppers – Cut to Matchstick Strips
- 3 Tbsp. of Red Curry Paste
- 2 Chicken Breasts – Boneless, Skinless – Slice Thin
- 2 Cups of Coconut Milk
- ¼ Cup of Basil Leaves
- Quinoa – Cooked

Directions:

1. Heat the oil in a large pan on medium heat.
2. Add in the onions, the yellow pepper, and the red peppers. Sauté them. Stir frequently. It will take about 5 minutes.
3. Add in the curry paste and cook it for 1 minute.
4. Add in the coconut milk, bring it to a boil on low heat and simmer it until the vegetables are

soft and the chicken s thoroughly cooked. It will take about 10 minutes.

5. Add in the basil leaves. Serve it with cucumber salad and quinoa.

Nutritional Information:

- Calories: 620
- Total Fat: 54g
- Saturated Fat: 46g
- Carbohydrates: 15g
- Protein: 24g

Crockpot Red Lentil Curry

Ingredients:

- 2 Cups of Red Lentils
- 1 Onion – Chopped
- 1 Clove of Garlic – Minced
- 1 tsp. of Ginger – Ground
- ½ tsp. of Cumin
- 3 Tbsp. of Red Curry Paste
- 2 tsp. of Garam Masala
- ½ tsp. of Turmeric
- 25 Ounces of Tomato Puree
- 1 tsp. of Salt
- ¼ Cup of Coconut Milk
- Green Onions – Chopped, Garnish

Garam Masala

- ½ tsp. of Coriander

- ¼ tsp. of Cardamon

- ½ tsp. of Pepper

- ¼ tsp. of Cinnamon

- ¼ tsp. of Cloves

- ¼ tsp. of Nutmeg

Directions:

1. Rinse your lentils and throw away the bad ones.

2. Add the garlic, ginger, onions, curry past, cumin, garam masala, and the turmeric into the slow cooker. Stir it well.

3. Pour in the tomatoes on the lentil mix. Add in 25 Ounces of water and stir it.

4. Cover it and cook it on low for 6 hours. Add in the salt and the coconut milk before you serve it.

5. Serve it on brown rice or some quinoa.

Nutritional Information:

- Calories: 199
- Total Fat: 3g
- Saturated Fat: 1g
- Carbohydrates: 31g
- Protein: 12g

Coconut Shrimp and Spicy Peach Dip

Ingredients:

- 2 Eggs
- ¼ Cup of Coconut Flour
- ¼ tsp. of Cayenne Pepper
- ¼ tsp. of Salt
- ¼ tsp. of Paprika
- ½ Cup of Panko Breadcrumbs
- ½ Cup of Shredded Coconut
- 1 Pound of Shrimp – Deveined, Tails On
- Coconut Oil

Directions:

1. Add in the eggs to a medium sized mixing bowl and whisk them together. Set it aside.
2. Add in the coconut flour, salt, paprika, and the cayenne pepper. Set it aside.
3. Add in the crumbs and the shredded coconut to a medium sized bowl. Put it aside.
4. Pick the shrimp up by the tail and dip them in the flour mix.

5. Dip them in the egg bowl, drip the egg-drenched shrimp in the coconut mix. Make sure it is coated well.

6. Repeat the process until all of your shrimp are covered.

7. Add 3 Tbsp. of coconut oil in a medium sized pan. Allow it to heat up for 3 minutes on medium low heat.

8. Transfer the shrimp to the pan, working in batches. Cook them for 2 minutes on each side.

9. Move the shrimp to a plate that is lined with a paper towel.

Nutritional Information:

- Calories: 440
- Total Fat: 16g
- Saturated Fat: 7g
- Carbohydrates: 20g
- Protein: 53g

Coconut Curry Crispy Fried Chicken

Ingredients:

- 14 Ounces of Coconut Milk
- 1 Tbsp. of Curry Powder
- 2 tsp. of Curry Powder
- 8 Chicken pieces – Rinsed, Patted Dry
- 1 tsp. of Salt – Divided
- ½ tsp. of Pepper
- 2 Cups of Flour
- Oil to Fry

Directions:

1. Combine the coconut milk, ½ tsp. of salt, and 1 Tbsp. of curry powder in a mixing bowl.
2. Put the rest of the curry powder, pepper, salt, and flour in a plastic bag.
3. Remove the chicken from the milk and put it in the bag. Toss it to coat the chicken. Allow it to set for 15 minutes.
4. Heat 1 inch of oil in a pan on medium heat until it is 350 degrees Fahrenheit.

5. Remove the chicken from the flour and shake off the excess. Fry it in the oil for 5 minutes.
6. Reduce the heat to a medium low and cook it for another 20-30 minutes or until the juices run clear.

Nutritional Information:

- Calories: 830
- Total Fat: 52g
- Saturated Fat: 27g
- Carbohydrates: 54g
- Protein: 37g

Teriyaki Coconut Chicken

Ingredients:

- 4 Chicken Breasts – Boneless, Skinless
- 1 Teriyaki Sauce
- 1 Tbsp. of Coconut Oil
- 2 Cups of Cooked Rice

Directions:

1. Add the chicken to a large zip lock bag.
2. Pour in half of the teriyaki sauce on the chicken.
3. Press out as much of the air as possible. Seal the bag.
4. Toss your chicken to ensure that it is well coated. Refrigerate for 6-8 hours.
5. Drizzle the oil on the medium pan on the medium low heat.
6. Add the chicken to the pan, stirring it frequently. Cook it until it is tender. This will take 8-10 minutes.
7. Add more teriyaki sauce in with the chicken. Reserve approximately ¼ cup for the serving.

8. Toss it to coat it well and then serve on top of
   the rice.

Nutritional Information:
- Calories: 650
- Total Fat: 17g
- Saturated Fat: 6g
- Carbohydrates: 92g
- Protein: 31g

Spaghetti Squash and Shrimp Pesto

Ingredients:

- 1 Spaghetti Squash
- 1 Pound of Shrimp – Peeled, Deveined
- 1 Tbsp. of Coconut Oil
- Dash of Salt
- Dash of Pepper
- Pesto

Directions:

1. Slice the squash in half, lengthwise.
2. Chop the ends off. Put both of the halves face down.
3. Put an inch of water in the pan.
4. Microwave it for 15 minutes.
5. Turn the dish at the halfway mark. It is done when the fork can easily go through the skin.
6. Heat a medium sized pan with the oil. Wash and dry the shrimp thoroughly.
7. Season it with pepper and salt.

8. Add it to the pan and cook the shrimp on each side for 3-5 minutes.

9. Once the squash is cooled down a bit, take a fork and run it through the inside to make strands.

10. Continue it until you hit the skin.

11. Put the squash in a bowl; top it with shrimp and the pesto.

Nutritional Information:

- Calories: 260
- Total Fat: 9g
- Saturated Fat: 3g
- Carbohydrates: 27g
- Protein: 26g

Coconut Chicken and Spinach

Ingredients:

- 1 Chicken Breast
- 3 Cups of Baby Spinach
- 1 Large Onion – Chopped
- ½ Cup of Coconut Milk
- 3 Tbsp. of Coconut Oil
- 1 Handful of Almonds
- Salt
- Pepper

Directions:

1. Chop the almonds in a food processor. Lightly brown them in a pan with the coconut oil. Put them aside.
2. Add in the coconut milk and the spinach to a medium sized pot. Cover it and allow it to simmer on low heat.
3. Sauté the onions in a pan for about 2 minutes.
4. Cut the chicken into squares.
5. Add it to a pan and leave it to thoroughly cook.

6. Take your chicken and the onions, and add in the pot with the coconut milk and the spinach. Stir it and cover it for 2 minutes.

7. Serve it with the almonds as garnish.

Nutritional Information:

- Calories: 630
- Total Fat: 54g
- Saturated Fat: 32g
- Carbohydrates: 22g
- Protein: 24g

Peanut and Coconut Chili Chicken

Ingredients:

- 2 Tbsp. of Cooking Oil
- 1 Large Yellow Onion – Chopped
- 2 Cloves of Garlic – Minced
- 1 Inch of Ginger Root – Minced
- 1 Pound of Chicken Breasts – Cut to Bite Size
- ¼ Cup of Chili Sauce
- 3 Tbsp. of Chunky Peanut Butter
- 3 Tbsp. of Chili Powder
- 1 tsp. of Brown Sugar
- 14 Ounces of Coconut Milk – Unsweetened
- 1 tsp. of Salt
- Cilantro – Fresh, Chopped, Garnish
- Roasted Peanuts – Chopped, Garnish

Directions:

1. Heat the oil in a medium sized pan on medium high heat.

2. Cook the onions until they are soft. It will take 5 minutes.

3. Add in the garlic and the ginger. Cook it for another 2 minutes.

4. Add in the chicken and cook it for 3-4 minutes.

5. Add in the chili sauce, peanut butter, chili powder, and sugar. Stir it well.

6. Add the coconut milk and the salt. Bring it to boil.

7. Reduce the heat to medium low. Cover it and simmer it for 20 minutes.

8. Add salt.

9. Serve it on rice. Garnish it with cilantro and the peanuts.

Nutritional Information:

- Calories: 530
- Total Fat: 40g
- Saturated Fat: 23g
- Carbohydrates: 17g
- Protein: 30g

Slow Cooked Peanut Butter Chicken with Ramen Noodles

Ingredients:

- 1 Tbsp. of Soy Sauce
- 13 ½ Ounces of Coconut Milk – Light
- ½ Cup of Creamy Peanut Butter – Reduced Fat
- 1 tsp. of Chili Powder
- 1 tsp. of Minced Garlic
- 1 Green Bell Pepper – Stemmed, Seeded, Sliced
- 1 Red Bell Pepper – Stemmed, Seeded, Sliced
- ½ Cup of Beansprouts
- 2 Pounds of Chicken Breasts – Boneless, Skinless
- 6 Ounces of Ramen Noodles
- 2 Green Onions – Chopped

Directions:

1. Combine the soy sauce, peanut butter, coconut milk, and chili powder with 2 cups of water in your large slow cooker.

2. Stir in the garlic, red pepper, green pepper, bean sprouts, and the diced chicken.

3. Cook it on low for 6 to 8 hours or until the chicken is fully cooked.

4. Stir in the ramen noodles and put the packets aside.

5. Increase the heat to high and cook it for another 10-15 minutes until the noodles is soft. Add in the seasoning packets.

6. Garnish it with the green onions.

Nutritional Information:

- Calories: 390
- Total Fat: 21g
- Saturated Fat: 15g
- Carbohydrates: 21g
- Protein: 31g

Paleo Basil with Avocado Zucchini Pasta

Ingredients:

- 5 Small Zucchinis
- 3 Avocados
- ¾ Cup of Fresh Basil Leaves – Chopped
- 1 tsp. of Sea Salt
- 3 tsp. of Garlic Powder
- 3 Tbsp. of Extra Virgin Olive Oil
- ½ Lemon
- 2 Tbsp. of Coconut Oil
- 2 tsp. of Onion Powder
- 3 Strips of Cooked Bacon – Chopped

Directions:

1. Cut the zucchini into noodles.
2. Put the zucchini in your strainer.

3. Grind 4-5 twists of the sea salt on it.

4. Allow it to sit for 20 minutes.

5. Wrap the zucchini noodles in a cheesecloth or paper towels. Squeeze them gently. Put them aside.

6. Put the avocados, 1 tsp. of sea salt, basil, olive oil, garlic, and lemon juice in a food processor. Blend it until it is smooth.

7. Heat the coconut oil in a pan on medium heat.

8. Add in the zucchini noodles and the onion to sauté it for 2-3 minutes.

9. Add in the avocado sauce and toss it to coat it.

10. Stir it and top it with the bacon pieces.

Nutritional Information:

- Calories: 470
- Total Fat: 42g
- Saturated Fat: 11g
- Carbohydrates: 24g
- Protein: 7g

Ginataang Langka and Pork

Ingredients:

- 20 Ounces of Jackfruit – Unripe, Chopped
- 10 Ounces of Pork – Cubed
- 2 Cups of Coconut Milk
- 4 Pieces of Chili Pepper – Chopped
- 1 Medium Sized Onion – Sliced Thin
- 1 tsp. of Minced Garlic
- 1 Tbsp. of Fish Sauce
- ¼ tsp. of Pepper
- 2 Tbsp. of Cooking Oil

Directions:

1. Heat the oil in a pan.
2. When the oil gets hot, sauté the garlic and the onions.
3. Add in the pork. Cook it until it is medium brown.
4. Pour the coconut milk in your pan. Let it boil
5. Cover it and allow it to simmer for 20 minutes. Add water if it is needed.

6. Add in the pepper, fish sauce, chili, and then
   stir it.

7. Add the jackfruit and stir it for 5-7 minutes.

8. Transfer it to a bowl.

Nutritional Information:

- Calories: 514
- Total Fat: 51g
- Saturated Fat: 35g
- Carbohydrates: 32g
- Protein: 27g

Easy Balsamic Salmon

Ingredients:

- 2 Salmon Fillets
- ½ Tbsp. of Coconut Oil
- ½ Tbsp. of Honey
- 3 Tbsp. of Balsamic Vinegar
- 1 tsp. of Red Pepper Flakes
- Sea Salt
- Pepper

Directions:

1. Heat the oil in a large pan on medium to high heat.
2. Season both sides of the salmon with the salt and the pepper.
3. Add the salmon to the pan and cook it 1-2 minutes on each side until it is brown.
4. Whisk the honey, red pepper flakes, and vinegar in a small mixing bowl.

5. Add the vinegar mix to the pan and simmer it until the fish is tender. It will take about 5 minutes.

6. Reduce it to a simmer for 5-10 minutes.

Nutritional Information:

- Calories: 300
- Total Fat: 18g
- Saturated Fat: 6g
- Carbohydrates: 9g
- Protein: 23g

Check out our FREE newsletter for all kinds of great offers & deals! Like us on Facebook!

https://www.facebook.com/recipejunkies

Crusted Tilapia and Coconut Almonds

Ingredients:

- 1 Pound of Tilapia Fillets
- ¼ Cup of Almonds – Unsalted
- ¼ Cup of Dried Coconut Flakes – Unsweetened
- Dash of Salt
- Dash of Pepper
- 1 Spray of Olive Oil
- Parsley
- Garlic Salt

Directions:

1. Pre-heat your oven to 375 degrees Fahrenheit.
2. Line your baking sheet with liner or parchment paper.
3. Combine the coconut, almonds, parsley pepper, and salt.
4. Pulse it in a food processor until it is combined well. It should feel like breadcrumbs.
5. Lay your tilapia on the baking sheet.
6. Sprinkle it with garlic salt.

7. Sprinkle the coconut mix on the top of each piece of fish.

8. Spray the fish with olive oil.

9. Bake it for 20 minutes until it is browned and flakey.

Nutritional Information:

- Calories: 424
- Total Fat: 22g
- Saturated Fat: 17g
- Carbohydrates: 10g
- Protein: 49g

Paleo Shepherds Pie

Ingredients:

- 1 Pound of Lamb or Beef – Ground
- 1 Medium Zucchini – Chopped
- 1 Yellow Squash – Chopped
- 4 Medium Sized Sweet Potatoes – Chunked
- ½ Cup of Coconut Milk
- Chili Powder
- Garlic Powder
- Salt
- Pepper

Directions:

1. Preheat your oven to 350 degrees Fahrenheit.
2. Heat the coconut oil in a large pan on medium high heat.
3. Add the ground meat and cook it for 10 minutes.
4. Add in the chopped zucchini and the yellow squash along with all the spices too the meat. Cook it for another 10 minutes.

5. Bring a pot of water to a boil and add in the sweet potatoes.

6. Cook them for 20-25 minutes until they are cooked.

7. Drain and mash it with the coconut milk, pepper, and salt.

8. Put the meat and the vegetables in a 9x13 pan.

9. Layer the mashed potatoes on the top.

10. Put it in the oven and cook it for 15 minutes.

Nutritional Information:

- Calories: 540
- Total Fat: 34g
- Saturated Fat: 18g
- Carbohydrates: 35g
- Protein: 25g

Spinach Coconut Curry

Ingredients:

- Extra Virgin Olive Oil
- 2 Spring Onions – Sliced
- 2 Tbsp. of Curry Paste
- 17 Ounces of Chicken Breasts
- 13 Ounces of Pumpkin – Cut to Cubes
- 13 Ounces of Coconut Cream
- 13 Ounces of Fresh Spinach – Chopped

Directions:

1. Heat the oil in a large pan and cook it gently with the spring onions and the curry paste.
2. Add the chicken breast and stir the chunks of chicken until it is browned.
3. Add in the coconut cream and the pumpkin cubes. Mix it gently.
4. Cover the pan with a lid and allow it to simmer on low for 20 minutes.
5. Stir it occasionally.

6. Before you serve it, add in the chopped spinach and stir it gently for 2-3 minutes.

7. Serve it with the coconut threads on the top.

Nutritional Information:

- Calories: 460
- Total Fat: 35g
- Saturated Fat: 27g
- Carbohydrates: 16g
- Protein: 28g

Pina Colada Pork Chops

Ingredients:

- 4 Pork Loin Chops
- 3 Limes
- ½ Cup of Coconut Milk
- Salt
- Cayenne Pepper
- 4 Scallions – Minced
- ½ Cup of Cilantro – Minced

Directions:

1. Marinate your pork in the juice from one lime.
2. Prepare a medium hot fire.
3. Grill the chops on indirect heat for about 6-8 minutes on each side. The internal temperature should reach at least 145 degrees Fahrenheit. Set them aside for 3 minutes.
4. Warm the coconut milk on low heat and season it with salt and cayenne pepper.
5. Add the juice from the second lime into your sauce.

6. Transfer the chops to a platter when they are done.

7. Spoon the sauce on the chops.

8. Garnish it with scallions and cilantro.

9. Sprinkle the juice from the third lime on the top and serve it with rice.

Nutritional Information:

- Calories: 380
- Total Fat: 17g
- Saturated Fat: 9g
- Carbohydrates: 13g
- Protein: 50g

Chicken Verde Enchiladas

Ingredients:

- 3 Chicken Breasts
- 2 Tbsp. of Butter
- ½ Cup of Salsa Verde
- 3 Tbsp. of Chicken Broth
- 1 tsp. of salt
- ½ tsp. of Pepper
- 14 Corn Tortillas
- ¼ Cup of Coconut Oil
- ¾ Cup of Salsa Verde
- 1 ½ Cups of Mozzarella Cheese
- Jack Cheese

Directions:

1. Put the chicken, butter, salsa, broth, salt, and the pepper in the crock pot.
2. Turn your crock pot to high and allow it to cook for 4 hours or on low for 6-8 hours.

3. During the last 30 minutes of the cooking, shred the chicken and allow it to cook for 30 minutes.

4. Preheat your oven to 350 degrees Fahrenheit.

5. Spray a 9x13 inch pan and a 9-inch pan with cooking spray.

6. Take each of the tortillas and dip it into the melted coconut oil.

7. Fill each of the tortilla with the chicken and put them into one of the baking dishes.

8. Once the tortillas are filled, pour the salsa over the enchiladas to cover them completely.

9. Top it with the cheese and bake it with aluminum foil on top for 25-30 minutes.

Nutritional Information:

- Calories: 370
- Total Fat: 20g
- Saturated Fat: 13g
- Carbohydrates: 29g
- Protein: 19g

Tomato Basil Coconut Chicken

Ingredients:

- 4 Chicken Breasts
- 2 Tbsp. of Butter
- 1 Cup of Cherry Tomatoes – Halved
- 4 Large Basil Leaves – Sliced
- 2 Cloves of Garlic – Minced

Directions:

1. Heat butter on medium high heat.
2. Add in the chicken breasts to the large pan.
3. Add in the tomatoes.
4. Cook the chicken for 3 minutes on both sides. Ensure that it is completely done.
5. During the last minute, add in the basil and the garlic. Toss it.

Nutritional Information:

- Calories: 600
- Total Fat: 45g
- Saturated Fat: 16g
- Carbohydrates: 5g
- Protein: 40g

Teriyaki Salmon

Ingredients:

- 2 Salmon Fillets
- 2 Tbsp. of Coconut Aminos
- 1 Tbsp. of Brown Sugar
- 1 Lemon
- 1 Tbsp. of Extra Virgin Olive Oil
- 1 Tbsp. of Ginger – Finely Chopped

Directions:

1. Mix all of the ingredients together, except for the salmon.
2. Put the fillets into an oven dish and cover it with the marinade.
3. Spoon it over the fish a few times. Cover it with foil.

4. Bake it for 20 minutes on 355 degrees Fahrenheit.

Nutritional Information:

- Calories: 160
- Total Fat: 11g
- Saturated Fat: 2g
- Carbohydrates: 5g
- Protein: 12g

Coconut Curried Rice

Ingredients:

- 1 Cup of Basmati Rice
- 14 Ounces of Coconut Milk – Light
- ¾ Cup of Water
- 1 Tbsp. of Virgin Coconut Oil
- 1 tsp. of Salt
- 2 tsp. of Virgin Coconut Oil
- 2 Cloves of Garlic – Crushed
- 1 Red Chili Peppers – Finely Chopped
- 1 Medium Sized Onion – Chopped
- 1 tsp. of Cumin Seed
- 1 Carrot – Chopped
- ½ Cup of Sweet Corn
- ½ Cup of Peas
- ½ Cup of Beansprouts
- ½ tsp. of Turmeric
- ½ tsp. of Coriander – Ground
- ½ tsp. Garam Masala
- 1 Tbsp. of Curry Powder

- 1 tsp. of Cumin

- ½ tsp. of Chilies – Puree

- Dash of Pepper

Directions:

1. Prepare the rice. Add the water, coconut milk, coconut oil, and the salt to a pan and bring it to a boil on medium heat.
2. Once it boils, add in the rice. Allow it to cook until it is done.
3. When the rice has 5 minutes left, add in the rest of the ingredients. Stir it all together.

Nutritional Information:

- Calories: 410

- Total Fat: 25g

- Saturated Fat: 25g

- Carbohydrates: 44g

- Protein: 6g

Saucy Coconut Green Beans and Chicken

Ingredients:

- 1 ½ Pounds of Chicken Breasts – Boneless, Skinless
- 2 Pounds of Green Beans – Trimmed, Cut to 2 inch Pieces
- 2 Tbsp. of Avocado Oil – Divided
- 25 Ounces of Tomato Sauce
- 6 Ounces of Tomato Paste
- 2 Tbsp. of Parsley – Chopped Fine

Directions:

1. Preheat your large pan on low to medium heat and add in 1 tablespoon of oil. Swirl it around to coat the pan.
2. Add in the chicken and cook it until it is done. Transfer it to a bowl and set it aside.
3. Add in the rest of the oil, swirl it to coat the pan and add in the green beans. Cover it and cook it for 10 minutes.

4. Add the chicken, tomatoes sauce, and the paste.
    Stir it.

5. Cover it and cook it for 5 minutes.

Nutritional Information:

- Calories: 520
- Total Fat: 17g
- Saturated Fat: 5g
- Carbohydrates: 9g
- Protein: 46g

Asian Paleo Chicken Meatballs and Teriyaki Glaze

Ingredients:

- 3 Pounds of Chicken Breasts – Boneless, Skinless – Cut to Chunks
- 2 Tbsp. of Coconut Oil
- 1 tsp. of Ginger – Ground
- 2 Tbsp. of Coconut Aminos
- 2 Cloves of Garlic – Minced
- 1 tsp. of Hot Red Pepper Flakes
- 1 Teriyaki Sauce
- 6 Green Onions
- Coconut Oil

Directions:

1. Combine your chicken, oil, ginger, garlic, coconut aminos, 3-4 green onions, and the pepper flakes in your food processor and pulse it until it is smooth.
2. Heat the oil in a pan on medium heat.
3. Form the chicken mix into balls that are golf ball sized

4. Cook them for 5-6 minutes on each side and then reduce the heat if you need too.

5. Once the meat is cooked, remove them from the pan and put them on a platter.

6. Drizzle the teriyaki sauce on top and top it with the rest of the green onions (chopped).

Nutritional Information:

- Calories: 460
- Total Fat: 17g
- Saturated Fat: 5g
- Carbohydrates: 3g
- Protein: 72g

Ribs in the Slow Cooker

Ingredients:

- 2 ½ Pounds of Beef Ribs
- 1 Batch of BBQ Sauce
- 1 Tbsp. of Paprika
- 1 Tbsp. of Coconut Sugar
- 1 tsp. of Sea Salt
- 1 tsp. of Pepper

Directions:

1. In a large pot, make the BBQ sauce as you were supposed to.
2. Mix the seasonings together. Rub the seasoning on the ribs.
3. Pour the sauce on the ribs and set it to cook for 6 hours.
4. Transfer them to a rack on the baking sheet and broil them on high for 2-3 minutes.
5. Take the rest of the sauce from the pot and heat it for 5-7 minutes and brush it on the ribs.
6. Cut the ribs and serve them.

Nutritional Information:

- Calories: 15
- Total Fat: 0g
- Saturated Fat: 0g
- Carbohydrates: 3g
- Protein: 13g

Coconut Sloppy Joe

Ingredients:

- 2 Tbsp. of Coconut Oil
- 1 Medium Bell Pepper – Any Color
- 1 Large Onion
- 1 tsp. of Salt
- 1 tsp. of Garlic Powder
- 1 Pound of Beef – Ground
- ¾ Cup of Ketchup
- ¼ Cup of Coconut Aminos
- 2 Tbsp. of Tomato Paste

Directions:

1. Put the coconut oil in a large pan.
2. Dice up the pepper and the onion and sauté them on medium heat.
3. Cook them for about 5 minutes.
4. Sprinkle it with salt and the garlic powder. Stir it.
5. Add in the beef and break it up using a spatula. Cook it until it is browned.

6. Add in the ketchup, tomato paste, and the coconut aminos. Stir it.

7. Let it cook on low for about 10 minutes.

8. Serve it over noodles or a sweet potato.

Nutritional Information:

- Calories: 110
- Total Fat: 5g
- Saturated Fat: 5g
- Carbohydrates: 14g
- Protein: 2g

Coconut Thai Rice

Ingredients:

- 1 Cup of Basmati Rice
- 14 Ounces of Coconut Milk
- ¼ Cup of Water
- ½ tsp. of Salt
- ½. Of Sugar
- ½ tsp. of Red Pepper Flakes
- 1/8 tsp. of Turmeric
- 1 tsp. of Ginger – Chopped

Directions:

1. Combine all of the ingredients in a pan.
2. Stir it well.
3. Cook it on medium high heat until it begins to boil
4. Reduce the heat to low.
5. Cover it and cook it for approximately 18 minutes.
6. Fluff it with a fork.
7. Cover it and allow it to stand for 5 minutes.

Nutritional Information:

- Calories: 174
- Total Fat: 0g
- Saturated Fat: 0g
- Carbohydrates: 37g
- Protein: 4g

Curry Soup with Coconut, Lime, and Chicken

Ingredients:

- 14 ½ Ounces of Chicken Broth – Reduced Sodium
- 14 Ounces of Coconut Milk – Unsweetened
- ½ Tbsp. of Curry Powder
- 1 Jalapeno Chile – Seeded, Minced
- 4 Chicken Breast – Boneless, Skinless, Halved
- 2 Tbsp. of Lime Juice
- Salt
- Pepper
- ¼ Cup of Green Onion – Chopped
- ¼ Cup of Cilantro – Chopped
- 1 Cup of Cooked White Rice
- Lime Wedge

Directions:

1. Bring the broth, curry powder, coconut milk, and chili to a simmer in a heavy pan on medium heat.

2. Add in the chicken and simmer it until it is cooked. It will take about 5 minutes.

3. Mix in the lime juice.

4. Season it with pepper and salt.

5. Divide the rice between dishes.

6. Ladle the soup on top.

7. Sprinkle it with the cilantro and green onions.

Nutritional Information:

- Calories: 110
- Total Fat: 3g
- Saturated Fat: 1g
- Carbohydrates: 15g
- Protein: 7g

Lime Coconut Shrimp

Ingredients:

- 3 Limes
- 2 Pounds of Shrimp – Peeled, Deveined
- 14 Ounces of Coconut Milk
- 1 Tbsp. of Salt
- ½ tsp. of Pepper
- 1/3 Cup of Coconut Flakes

Directions:

1. Use a greater to zest the limes and then set them aside.
2. Squeeze two limes and then combine the juice with the coconut milk and your shrimp. Refrigerate it for 15-30 minutes.
3. In the food processor, combine the lime zest, pepper, and the salt. Pulse it to blend it.
4. Remove your shrimp from the marinade and put them in

Nutritional Information:

- Calories: 206
- Total Fat: 10g
- Saturated Fat: 2g
- Carbohydrates: 10g
- Protein: 18g

Ginger and Coconut rice

Ingredients:

- 2 Cups of Chicken Broth
- ½ Cup of Coconut Milk – Reduced Fat
- 2 tsp. of Ginger – Grated
- 1 Cup of Rice – Uncooked
- ½ tsp. of Lemon Zest
- 2 Green Onions – Chopped
- 2 Tbsp. of Flaked Coconut – Toasted
- Lemon Slice for Garnishing

Directions:

1. Heat the broth, ginger, and coconut milk to a boil in a pan on medium high heat.
2. Stir in the rice.
3. Heat it to a boil and then reduce the heat.
4. Cover it and allow it to simmer for 15 minutes.
5. Add in the lemon zest and the green onions.
6. Fluff the rice with a fork.
7. Garnish it with coconut and the lemon slices.

Nutritional Information:

- Calories: 127
- Total Fat: 0g
- Saturated Fat: 0g
- Carbohydrates: 28g
- Protein: 2g

Coconut Thai Red Curry

Ingredients:

- 2 Tbsp. of Red Curry Paste
- 15 Ounces of Coconut Milk
- ¼ Cup of Basil
- ¼ Cup of Bamboo Shoot
- 3 tsp. of Fish Sauce
- 2 Tbsp. of Brown Sugar
- 1/3 Cup of Chicken Stock
- ½ Cup of Mushrooms
- ½ Red Bell Pepper
- ½ Green Pepper
- ½ Yellow Pepper
- ½ Onion
- 2 Chicken Breasts
- 10 Ounces of Brown Rice

Directions:

1. In a medium pan combine ½ to 1 tablespoon of red curry paste with the coconut milk.

2. Simmer it for 5 minutes.

3. Add in ¼ cup of basil, ¼ cup of bamboo shoots, 2 tablespoons of brown sugar, 3 teaspoons of fish sauce, 1/3 cup of chicken stock, and ½ cup of mushrooms. Simmer it for 10-15 minutes.

4. Sauté the peppers in a different pan with the chopped onion and oil. Fry them lightly with the chicken breasts until it hey are cooked.

5. Put the sautéed peppers and the onions on top of the rice and spoon on the curry sauce with the rice.

Nutritional Information:

- Calories: 650
- Total Fat: 17g
- Saturated Fat: 17g
- Carbohydrates: 92g
- Protein: 31g

Curried Coconut Chicken

Ingredients:

- 1 Tbsp. of Curry Powder
- ½ tsp. of Salt
- 2 tsp. of Coconut Oil
- 2 Cloves of Garlic – Minced
- 2 tsp. of Minced Ginger
- 1 Cup of Onion – Chopped
- 1 Pound of Chicken Breast – Boneless, Cubed
- ½ Cup of Coconut Milk – Low Fat
- 1 Tbsp. of Lime Juice

Directions:

1. Combine your curry powder and the salt in a bowl.
2. Add in the chicken and toss it to coat it.
3. Heat he oil in a pan on medium high heat.
4. Add in the ginger, garlic, and the onion.
5. Cook it for 1 minute.
6. Add in the chicken and sear it for 2-3 minutes on each side.

7. Add in the coconut milk and the lime juice.

8. Reduce the heat to medium and cook it for 15 minutes.

Nutritional Information:

- Calories: 650
- Total Fat: 17g
- Saturated Fat: 6g
- Carbohydrates: 92g
- Protein: 31g

Coconut Shrimp with Sweet and Sour Sauce

Ingredients:

- ½ Cup of Flour
- ½ tsp. of Baking Powder
- ½ tsp. of Paprika
- ½ tsp. of Seasoned Salt
- 2/33 Cup of Water
- ½ Cup of Bread Crumbs
- 2 Cups of Shredded Coconut
- 1 Pound of Shrimp – Deveined, Peeled

Sauce

- 20 Ounces of Pineapples Chunks with the Juice
- 3 Cloves of Garlic – Peeled
- 2 Tbsp. of Soy Sauce
- 2 Tbsp. of Corn Starch
- 1 Jalapeno Pepper
- 1 Red Bell Pepper
- 2 Tbsp. of Cider Vinegar

Directions:

1. Remove the seeds and the cores from your peppers.
2. Prepare the sauce by blending all of the ingredients together in a blender.
3. Simmer it on low heist for 15 minutes. Stir in the vinegar.
4. Heat 1 inch of the coconut oil in a heavy pan to 365 degrees Fahrenheit.
5. Using a whisk, stir the flour, baking powder, salt, and paprika in a bowl.
6. Add in the water and whisk it until the batter is very smooth. Put it aside.
7. In a different bowl, mix the breadcrumbs and the coconut to make a coating for the shrimp.
8. One by one, add the shrimp to the batter and then roll it in the coconut mix.
9. When the oil is hot, fry the shrimp in batches until they are golden brown. Turn the shrimp once.
10.   Remove it from the oil with a slotted spoon. Allow them to drain on paper towels.

Nutritional Information:

- Calories: 74
- Total Fat: 2g
- Saturated Fat: 1g
- Carbohydrates: 5g
- Protein: 3g

Coconut Sweet Potato Coconut Casserole

Ingredients:

- 3 Cups of Sweet Potatoes – Mashed
- 1 ½ Cups of Sugar
- 4 Eggs – Beaten
- 1 tsp. of Vanilla
- 1 tsp. of Dark Rum
- 1 tsp. of Lemon Juice
- ½ tsp. of Nutmeg
- 1 tsp. of Cinnamon
- Dash of Salt
- 2 ½ Cups of Milk
- 1 Stick of Butter
- 1 Cup of Flaked Coconut

Directions:

1. Wash and peel the potatoes. Cut them into chunks and boil them in salted water.
2. Mash them with the butter when they are hot.
3. Stir in the sugar, lemon, vanilla, and the seasonings.
4. Beet the eggs very well and combine it with the milk.
5. Add the coconut in and stir it well.
6. Slowly add the milk/coconut mix into the sweet potatoes and stir it well.
7. Butter a casserole dish and transfer the potato mix into the dish evenly.
8. Dot the top with butter.
9. Bake it at 400 degrees Fahrenheit until it is lightly browned on the top.

Nutritional Information:

- Calories: 228
- Total Fat: 0g
- Saturated Fat: 0g
- Carbohydrates: 48g
- Protein: 2g

Coconut Catfish Soup

Ingredients:

- ½ Pound of Catfish – 1 inch Chunks, Deboned
- 2 Cups of Fish Stock
- 1 Cup of Coconut Milk
- 1 Tbsp. of Lemon Grass – Sliced Thin
- 1 Tbsp. of Cilantro Leaves
- 1 Tbsp. of Thai Chile Peppers – Sliced Thin
- 1 Tbsp. of Galangal – Sliced Thin
- 1 Clove of Garlic – Minced
- 4 Tbsp. of Fish Sauce
- 4 Tbsp. of Lime Juice

Directions:

1. Combine all of the ingredients except for the fish and the coconut milk into a stockpot.
2. Bring it to a boil for at least 1 minute.
3. Reduce the heat and simmer it on low for 5 minutes.
4. Add in the coconut milk and the fish.
5. Simmer it for 10 minutes.

Nutritional Information:

- Calories: 201
- Total Fat: 12g
- Saturated Fat: 3g
- Carbohydrates: 7g
- Protein: 16g

Coconut Cheese Log

Ingredients:

- 4 Ounces of Bleu Cheese – Crumbled
- 8 Ounces of Cream Cheese – Soft
- ¾ tsp. of Dry Mustard
- 1 ½ Cups of Coconut Flakes – Toasted

Directions:

1. Cream the bleu cheese and the cream cheese together until it is soft.
2. Add in the dry mustard and mix it well.
3. Refrigerate it for 30 minutes.
4. Shape it into a log.
5. Roll it in the coconut.
6. Cut the log into ¼ inch slices.
7. Serve it with fruit or some crackers.

Nutritional Information:

- Calories: 794
- Total Fat: 79g
- Saturated Fat: 45g
- Carbohydrates: 9g
- Protein: 14g

Sticky Coconut Rice

Ingredients:

- 1 Cup of Pina Colada Drink Mixture
- 1 Can of Coconut Milk
- 2 Tbsp. of Sugar
- ½ tsp. of Salt
- 2 Cups of Water
- 2 ¼ Cups of Short Grain Rice
- ¼ Cup of Crushed Pineapple

Directions:

1. Bring the drink mix, coconut milk, the salt, and the water to a slow boil.
2. Stir in the rice and reduce the heat. Cover it and simmer it on low for 30 minutes.
3. Gently stir in the pineapple and fluff it with a fork.

Nutritional Information:

- Calories: 85
- Total Fat: 1g
- Saturated Fat: 0g

Carbohydrates: 18g Protein: 7g

Breaded Coconut Fish

Ingredients:

- 1 Pound of Fish – Tilapia, River Fish, Etc.
- ½ Pound of Shredded Coconut
- ½ Cup of Coconut Oil
- 1 Box of Crackers – Ritz
- 1 tsp. of Salt
- 1 tsp. of Pepper

Directions:

1. Preheat your oven to 400 degrees Fahrenheit.
2. In a zip lock bag, put the fish and ¼ cup of oil in and allow it to sit while you grind the crackers to powder.
3. Add in the coconut, pepper, and the salt.
4. Add the dry mix to the bag and shake it.
5. In a baking dish, use the rest of the oil and scoop out enough of the extra mix to put on the bottom of the dish.
6. Layer your fish and cover it with the rest of the dry mix.

7. Put dish in the oven for 20-30 minutes and cook it on each side until it is brown.

Nutritional Information:

- Calories: 47
- Total Fat: 2g
- Saturated Fat: 0g
- Carbohydrates: 1g
- Protein: 7g

Sour Cream Coconut Cake

Ingredients:

- 1 Package of Yellow Butter Cake Mix
- 2 Cups of Sugar
- 16 Ounces of Sour Cream
- 10 Ounces of Whipped Topping – Thawed
- 12 Ounces of Frozen Coconut – Thawed

Directions:

1. Prepare the cake as said on the package.
2. Bake it in 2 layers.
3. Once the cake is cool, split the layers in half.
4. Combine the sugar, coconut, and sour cream. Blend it very well
5. Save 1 cup of the mixture.
6. Spread the remaining mix on between the layers.
7. Combine the cup of the sour cream mix with the whipped topping.
8. Spread it on the top and the sides of the cake.
9. Refrigerate it for 3 days before you eat it.

Nutritional Information:

- Calories: 240
- Total Fat: 10g
- Saturated Fat: 3g
- Carbohydrates: 35g
- Protein: 1g

Coconut 5-Minute Pie

Ingredients:

- 3 Ounces of Cream Cheese
- 1 Tbsp. of Sugar
- ½ Cup of Milk
- 1 1/3 Cup of Angel Flake Coconut
- 3 ½ Cup of Cool Whip
- ½ tsp. of Almond Extract
- 8-9 inch Graham Cracker Crust

Directions:

1. Beat the cheese with an electric mixer.
2. Beat in the sugar.
3. Add the milk and fold in the coconut.
4. Add in the cool whip and the extract.
5. Spoon it into the crust.
6. Freeze it until it is firm.
7. Allow it to stand for 15 minutes before you cut it.

Nutritional Information:

- Calories: 270
- Total Fat: 14g
- Saturated Fat: 6g
- Carbohydrates: 31g
- Protein: 6g

Coconut Almond Coconut Cookies

Ingredients:

- 1 ½ Cup of Sugar
- 1 Cup of Butter
- 2 Eggs – Separated, Save the Whites
- ¾ Cup of Almonds – Chopped
- 2 tsp. of Cream of Tartar
- 2 ½ Cup of Flour
- 1 tsp. of Baking Soda
- ½ tsp. of Almond Extract
- 1-3 Cups of Coconut

Directions:

1. Mix all of the ingredients together in a large mixing bowl.
2. Roll them into balls and dip them into the egg whites.
3. Dip them into the coconut and then place them on an ungreased baking sheet.
4. Bake them at 350 degrees Fahrenheit for 10 minutes.

Nutritional Information:

- Calories: 97
- Total Fat: 3g
- Saturated Fat: 3g
- Carbohydrates: 17g
- Protein: 1g

Coconut Cream Pie

Ingredients:

- 2 Cups of Milk
- ¾ Cup of Sugar
- ½ Cup of Bisquick Mix
- 4 Eggs
- ¼ Cup of Butter
- 1 ½ tsp. of Vanilla
- 1 Cup of Coconut

Directions:

1. Combine all of the ingredients except for the coconut. Add to a blender and blend them for 3 minutes.

2. Pour it into a dish that is sprayed with cooking spray.

3. Let it stand for 5 minutes.

4. Sprinkle it with the coconut.

5. Bake it at 350 degrees Fahrenheit for 35-40 minutes.

Nutritional Information:

- Calories: 429
- Total Fat: 23g
- Saturated Fat: 10g
- Carbohydrates: 53g
- Protein: 3g

Chocolate Coconut Pie

Ingredients:

- 3 Squares of Chocolate – Unsweetened
- ½ Cup of Butter – Melted
- 3 Eggs
- ¾ Cup of Sugar
- ½ Cup of Flour
- 1 tsp. of Vanilla Extract
- 2/3 Cup of Sweetened Condensed Milk
- 2 2/3 Cup of Flaked Coconut

Directions:

1. Melt the chocolate and the butter together. Set it aside.
2. In our blender, put the eggs, flour, sugar, chocolate mix, and the vanilla and blend it on high for 1-2 minutes.
3. Pour it into a greased 9-inch pie pan.
4. Combine the sweetened milk and the coconut and spoon it over the pie filling. Leave ½ inch border around the edge.

5. Bake it on 350 degrees Fahrenheit for 30 minutes.

Nutritional Information:

- Calories: 380
- Total Fat: 18g
- Saturated Fat: 7g
- Carbohydrates: 50g
- Protein: 7g

Pina Colada (Can be made with no alcohol.)

Ingredients:

- ¼ Cup of Coconut Rum
- 1/3 Cup of Pineapple Juice
- 8 Ounces of Coconut Cream
- 8 Ounces of Pineapple Chunks
- Coconut Meat for Garnishing
- 11 Cubes of Ice

Directions:

1. Combine the juice and the rum in a bowl. Stir it for 30 seconds.
2. In the blender, combine the ice and the coconut cream. Blend it on high for 2 minutes.
3. Fold the coconut rum into the juice rum mix.

Nutritional Information:

- Calories: 245
- Total Fat: 3g
- Saturated Fat: 2g

- Carbohydrates: 32g
- Protein: 1g

Thank You!

13142110R00061

Printed in Great Britain
by Amazon.co.uk, Ltd.,
Marston Gate.